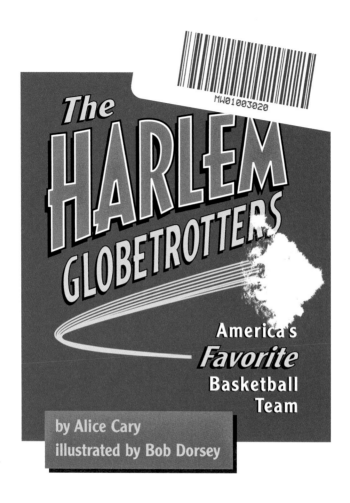

The HARLEM GLOBETROTTERS

America's *Favorite* Basketball Team

by Alice Cary
illustrated by Bob Dorsey

MODERN CURRICULUM PRESS

Pearson Learning Group

January 12, 1998, was a big day in Remington, Indiana. Cars jammed the high school parking lot and people, including reporters accompanied by TV cameras, crowded into the gym and waited. A letter from the President waited too!

The star basketball team took the court. On this day, the Harlem Globetrotters would play their 20,000th game. The crowd went wild with excitement.

No other professional sports team had ever played so many games. The Globetrotters had played before more people, and in more places, than any other team in the world.

This time the Globetrotters played the New York Nationals. As usual, the Globetrotters dazzled the crowd with their incredible skills. They handled the ball like magic and performed amazing tricks. As always, their fans laughed and cheered enthusiastically.

In that game, the Globetrotters beat the Nationals 85–62. In seventy-two seasons, the Globetrotters had attained a tremendous record of 19,668 wins and only 332 losses.

"This is our New Year's Eve, our birthday, our July Fourth, and our anniversary all rolled into one," said the team's owner.

How did this tremendous team get its start? Their story is one of dedication in the face of racial injustice.

Basketball began in 1891, but the National Basketball Association (NBA) didn't include African American players until 1950. That didn't stop the Globetrotters, though. They began as an African American team in the 1920s.

Now, years later, most people have heard of the Harlem Globetrotters, but few know that the team isn't, nor was it ever, from Harlem. In fact, the team almost stopped playing soon after it was formed.

The team's story began in Chicago in 1926 when twenty-four-year-old Abe Saperstein organized a team of African American basketball players. He called them the "Savoy Big Five."

The Savoy was a famous ballroom in Chicago. Its owners wanted more business, so the new team was invited to play there. It was hoped that people would watch the game and then stay to dance, but the plan didn't work. The games ended. So much for the team.

Saperstein decided to take some of his players on the road, crowding them all into his Model-T Ford. They wore uniforms that said "New York" on them, so people thought that's where they were from.

The team played its first game in Hinckley, Illinois, on January 7, 1927, for a crowd of three hundred people.

The players continued to tour the Midwest. In 1930, they changed their name to the Harlem Globetrotters, because Harlem was an area in New York City where many African Americans lived. The Globetrotters wanted everyone to know that they were African Americans who wanted to do their part to stop racial injustice. They were also globetrotters—they traveled all over.

The Globetrotters won game after game and traveled to new places every year. More and more people game to see them.

During one game in 1939, the team was ahead 112–5. One of the players grew bored, so he began to clown around on the court. The crowd loved his tricks.

After the game, Saperstein told his team they could continue to joke and clown around during games, but only if they were well ahead of the other team. Dedication and hard work still had to come first, after all.

A few years later, Reece "Goose" Tatum joined the team. Tatum was a super basketball player and a born comedian who invented tricks and pranks that made the Globetrotters even more famous.

In 1939, the Globetrotters suffered a minor disaster. In their first professional championship, they lost to another African American team, the New York Rens, who went on to win the championship.

The next year, however, the Globetrotters gave the Rens a jolt by beating them during another championship. Then they beat the Chicago Bruins in overtime, 31–29. Now the Globetrotters were the World Basketball Champions.

When they returned to Chicago after the championship, 22,000 people turned out to watch them play.

More and more people wanted to see the Harlem Globetrotters in action. Soon, *Life* magazine featured an article about them in 1946, and movies were made about their lives.

The team began to travel overseas. Now they were truly globetrotters because they went to Hawaii, Europe, and South America. Even the pope wanted to see them. Once they even played on the deck of a United States aircraft carrier.

The team became so popular that it stopped battles. In 1956, Peru was in the middle of a fierce civil war. Everyone stopped fighting for four days, though, to watch the Harlem Globetrotters play. As soon as the team left, the war resumed.

In one place, however, the crowd didn't cheer. The audience was absolutely quiet.

In 1949, the Globetrotters became the first professional basketball team to tour Alaska, traveling there by dog sled to play before a group of Inuits.

The team played well, doing their usual stunts and tricks, but the Inuits didn't laugh or clap. The crowd was completely silent. Later the Globetrotters learned an interesting thing about the Inuit culture—Inuits show their appreciation for something by being quiet.

At one point, the team had a serious problem. The players were so good that other teams didn't want to play them.

Team owner Abe Saperstein knew just what to do. He talked to his friend, Louis "Red" Klotz and convinced him to organize some new teams for the Globetrotters to play against.

Klotz did just that, creating new teams such as the Washington Generals, the Boston Shamrocks, and the Baltimore Rockets. Now the Globetrotters would be busy.

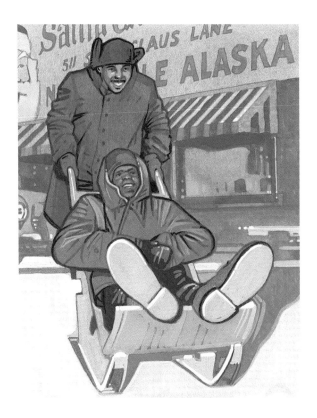

Over the years, some interesting players joined the Globetrotters. Two famous team "clowns" were George "Meadowlark" Lemon and "Curley" Neal, who made people laugh everywhere they went.

Wilt "The Stilt" Chamberlain joined the team in 1958. Some say he was basketball's greatest offensive player ever. He stayed with the team one year, and then joined the NBA.

The first woman joined the team in 1985. Expert ball handler Lynette Woodard played for several seasons, then she joined a team in Italy.

In 1997, team members Michael "Wild Thing" Wilson and Fred "Preacher" Smith set a new basketball world record. In England, they made a slam dunk of eleven feet, eleven inches!

Abe Saperstein died in 1966, at age sixty-three. He had been a tremendous leader for the team. In forty years, he had taken his players to 1,200 cities and 82 foreign countries where they had played nearly 8,945 games, with only 330 losses. Best of all, his players made people smile. No wonder everyone loved the Globetrotters.

The team's fame continued to grow. In 1970 a TV cartoon series called *The Harlem Globetrotters Show* began. It was a big hit and was the first time a sports team had such a show on TV.

Soon it seemed as if everyone wanted to be part of the act. When the leader of China visited the United States in 1979, he asked to meet the Globetrotters.

In 1982, the Globetrotters got their own star on Hollywood's Walk of Fame. Once again, they were the only sports team to receive such an honor.

n 1996, the team was seventy years old. To celebrate, they decided to do something very special.

The Globetrotters went to South Africa where there had been racial problems for many years. Now, though, South Africa was trying to resolve these problems and move closer to racial equality. The Globetrotters were the first professional basketball team to play in the new South Africa and raised over a million dollars to help children there.

A year later the Globetrotters were invited to return to South Africa to help celebrate President Nelson Mandela's seventy-ninth birthday.

The Globetrotters and Mandela were good partners, as both had spent years dedicating themselves to stamping out racial injustice.

Over the years, the Globetrotters have proved that they are indeed America's favorite basketball team.

How would you like to have a job where every day is different from the day before? A job where you make most of the day's decisions?

How would you like a job where you get to know every corner of your community? Where you meet famous people and have front-row seats to sports events and concerts?

How would you like to know the stories behind the events in the news? How would you like to help tell those stories?

But there's even more to this job. How would you feel about having to carry heavy equipment around eight hours a day? How would you like to work nights, weekends, and holidays and outside in weather that sends most people running for cover?

What if, to do a good job, you had to get close to dangerous fires and angry crowds?

How would you feel if your boss told you to take pictures of a tragic event at a clinic or on a roadside?

What if you were asked to work on a story about someone in trouble—maybe a person with a serious infection or someone who was homeless? What if you grew to know and care for that person? How would you feel?

PHOTO MAP OR ART REQUEST ASSIGNMENT

Photographer ....

Date .... Time .... ☐AM

If the good parts of this job sound exciting, and the bad parts sound OK, maybe you'd like to be a photojournalist.

A photojournalist is a photographer who takes pictures for news stories. Some photojournalists work for newspapers or magazines. Others sell their photographs to different news groups.

Photojournalists' pictures can be as beautiful as any work of art. But creating beauty is not the photojournalist's main goal. The goal is to provide information through interesting pictures.

For example, an art photographer might take a beautiful picture of a bridge at sunset. But a photojournalist might take a picture of workers inspecting the bridge in the morning.

This is Mara Lavitt. She has been a photojournalist for more than twenty years. Mara is a staff photographer for the *New Haven Register*, a newspaper in New Haven, Connecticut.

Mara loves her job. She has photographed governors, senators, two presidents, and many world leaders. She has photographed the New York Yankees, the New York Giants, and the Boston Bruins. She has also taken pictures of actors Tom Hanks, Eddie Murphy, and Jodie Foster, and singer Aretha Franklin.

Mara loves the challenge of working fast and accurately. She is used to the crazy hours. She doesn't even mind occasional discomfort.

This morning Mara's getting ready to go to work. She's saying good-by to her husband, Hayne, and her dog, Keta, before driving thirty miles to New Haven.

Mara is wearing warm clothes because it's a cold winter day. And chances are good that at least one of her assignments will be outside. She has on comfortable shoes because she'll be on her feet all day. Plus she never knows when she might need to dash across town to take a photograph.

She's carrying a change of clothes in her car in case she gets wet or dirty on the job. And she has her camera bag with all her equipment.

Mara carries two cameras. She uses one with a wide-angle lens when she wants to take a picture of a whole scene. She uses one with a telephoto lens when she needs to zoom in for a close-up. Each of her cameras is equipped with a motor drive. The motor drive advances film rapidly so she can take many photographs in quick succession.

Mara has several other camera lenses for special shots. She packs two kinds of film—one for indoor photographs and one for outdoor photographs. She also carries a flash and a battery to run it.

She always carries her reporter's notebook and pens so that she can jot down notes on each shot she takes. The best photograph in the world is no use to a newspaper if it lacks an accurate caption.

Mara's first stop of the day is the office of the *New Haven Register*. She goes to the clipboard in the Photography Department and takes down her assignments. On a typical day she'll take pictures for three different stories.

Each assignment is described on a different piece of paper. The sheet tells Mara where in the paper the story will appear—in News, Features, Sports, or Business. If Mara has any questions about an assignment, she asks the reporter who is writing the story.

Then it's time to hop in her car and get going again.

Using her assignment sheets and her maps, Mara plans out the day. She doesn't worry about getting lost because she knows New Haven and the surrounding towns well. She also knows the people who can steer her to what's happening—police officers on the beat, workers on the street, and neighborhood shop owners. Most assignments take between twenty minutes and one hour to complete. But things don't always go according to plan.

Sometimes her pager beeps, and Mara has to run to cover a breaking story. These stories are seldom happy ones. She might be called to the scene of a traffic accident or a fire. Pictures of a disaster are never easy for Mara to take, but she knows it's her responsibility to take them.

"I'm the eyes of the public. It's my job to show newspaper readers the world, and that includes tragedies."

When Mara was just starting out at the *Register*, she was called to the scene of an accident. A shed had collapsed on a man, and he was badly hurt. A helicopter had arrived to airlift the man. A surgeon was standing by at the hospital. Mara started to take pictures. A police officer who was standing by got very upset.

"How would you feel if that were your father?" he yelled.

Mara tried to explain that taking photographs wasn't a sign of disrespect. The officer allowed her to continue, but he clearly didn't approve.

Later, the victim of the accident died. For weeks, the words of the police officer echoed in Mara's head.

A month after the accident, Mara got a phone call that gave her a very different view of the incident.

"Hi," a woman said. "That was my father who died in the shed collapse. I'm trying to help my son understand what happened. I want him to know about all the people who tried to save his Grandpa. Your photographs did a really good job of showing how helpful people were. Do you have copies that you could send me?"

Mara did, and the woman was very grateful.

This experience taught Mara a lesson she has never forgotten: If you are a photojournalist, you have to accept that some people will love your work and some will hate it. Your job is to make each picture as honest as you can.

FEATURES PAGE

After Mara finishes shooting all of her day's assignments, she goes back to the newspaper. She pops her film into a machine. Twelve-and-a-half minutes later, color negatives come out.

Mara puts the negatives in a protective sleeve. Then she and the picture editor examine them. They pick the best photo for each story.

Mara scans the chosen photos into a computer. For each picture, she types in a caption. The caption tells who is in the photo, when and where the picture was taken, and what is happening in the shot.

Then Mara can go home for the day.

The next day, Mara sees her pictures in the newspaper and reads the stories that go with them. It's a source of pride for Mara to see one of her photographs on the front page.

If you ask Mara what it takes to be a good photojournalist, she will tell you that first, it takes curiosity.

Curiosity leads you to ask questions. The answers guide you to what's important. For example, if you're photographing a new fire station, talk to the firefighters first. Maybe one of them just received an award for bravery. Then you might want to put him or her in the foreground.

To take a good picture, you have to care about what you are photographing, whether it's a child running through a sprinkler or a surgeon working in a clinic.

Second, Mara's job takes dedication and determination. "You take shot after shot, and use up roll after roll of film. You don't stop until you get a photograph that readers will want to keep looking at," says Mara.

Third, photojournalism takes quick reflexes. Things happen fast, and the photojournalist has to react. If you're shooting a football player catching a pass or a police dog sniffing out a bomb, you may have only a second to click the shutter.

Fourth, the job requires technical knowledge. You have to understand photographic equipment, lighting, camera angles, and composition.

Last, being a good photojournalist takes experience. Experience helps you predict where the puck will go next in a hockey game. Experience tells you through which theater door the star will most likely come out. Experience teaches you how to get someone to relax for a portrait. It reminds you that a sad story requires a serious portrait, even if the person you are photographing has a beautiful smile.

If you think you might like to be a photojournalist, Mara has some suggestions.

"Start now. A simple camera is fine. Take pictures of your family and friends. Photograph school activities, such as science fairs or sports events. Work for the school newspaper, and try to take some photography classes. It can be a good idea to get a college diploma too."

"Experiment. Take pictures inside and outdoors. Try close-ups, medium shots, and long shots."

"Most of all, look! Look at the great photographs in newspapers and magazines and figure out what makes them effective. Look at people. Notice the way they lean forward when they're excited and cross their arms when they're uncomfortable. Pay attention to reflections in water and glass. Notice the way shadows fall across a building at the end of the day. Start to see the world in pictures. And then take them!"